bodies of water

bodies of water

CHEYENNE PETERSON

ReadersMagnet, LLC

Bodies of Water
Copyright © 2022 by *Cheyenne Peterson*

Published in the United States of America
ISBN   Paperback: 978-1-958030-28-8
ISBN   eBook: 978-1-958030-29-5

All rights reserved. No part of this publication may be reproduced, stored in a retrieval system or transmitted in any way by any means, electronic, mechanical, photocopy, recording or otherwise without the prior permission of the author except as provided by USA copyright law.

The opinions expressed by the author are not necessarily those of ReadersMagnet, LLC.

ReadersMagnet, LLC
10620 Treena Street, Suite 230 | San Diego, California, 92131 USA
1.619. 354. 2643 | www.readersmagnet.com

Book design copyright © 2022 by ReadersMagnet, LLC. All rights reserved.

Cover design by *Kent Chu*
Interior design by *Dorothy Lee*

*To each chapter, each body of water; youv'e swam through my heart and taken large gulps of my soul.
I hope the molecules of who I am still quench the thirst that vigorously raided all that you are.*

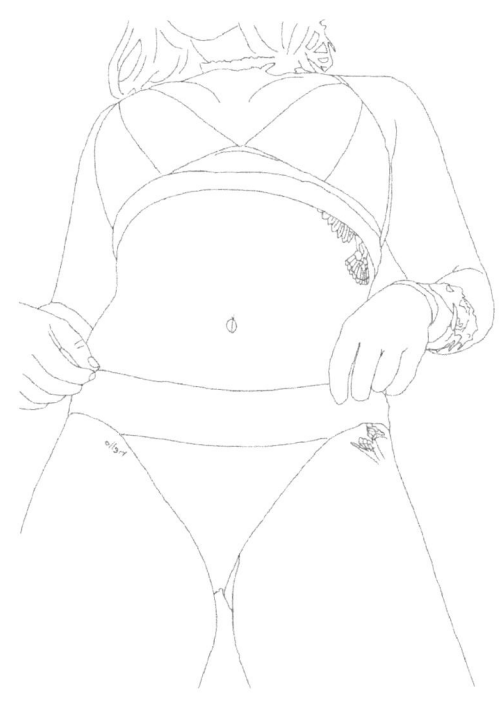

CONTENTS

Folly River

Impotent.	10
Overdose.	11
Estate.	12
Withdrawals.	13

Illicit Falls

Confessions.	16
Room #212.	17
To Her.	18
Aquatic Respiration.	19
Hymn of Love.	20
Taste of Poetry.	21
Wishful Wishing.	22
Toxic Blood, Clean Mind.	27
Serpentine.	28
Comparison Kills.	29

Trivial Pond

Worst Parts.	32
You Could Call This… Regret.	33

Insipid Stream

Hands.	36
Adrenaline Surge.	37
Writer's Block.	38
I shouldn't have let you in.	39

Celestial Tarn

Kissing; Exhaling. 43
Galaxy Merger. 44
Peruvian Love. 45

Pariah Delta

Grail. 48
The Night I Dreamt. 49
Your embodiment. 50
Contradictory. 51
Sanctuary. 52
Self Sever. 53

Deluges That Feed All

Lost and Free. 57
The Profound. 58
Unfortunately, My Future. 60
Stained. 63
My Monster Has a Name. 65
Paper Airplane. 66
Confluence. 67

Folly River

Foolishness, Stupidity, Idiocy.

Impotent.

We were meant for each other, once upon a time.
Now I lay here in this bed, lonelier next to you than before,
When I could touch each corner with my fingers and toes.
Thinking, 'How fast can I move out the endless closet of my wardrobe?'
Leave behind the shackled label of being your girlfriend.
Dash into the night, where stars acknowledge my presence.
Run away from the factory of thoughts that repeat,
'Is this the rest of my life?'
But I am afraid of the dark, and no longer a runner.
So, I'll lie in this bed, one night longer,
until the stars call my name,
Or the moon craves my textured skin.
But those are fantasies from the person I long to be.

Overdose.

The love you give me,
Drugging me.
Killing me slowly, while getting that *high*.
Never knowing the damage caused under the skin.
Let's pay attention to the *high*.
Soaring in the sky, with lust in my hair.
Crashing is inevitable, as you're not the best pilot.
Rough landings to end the *highs*.

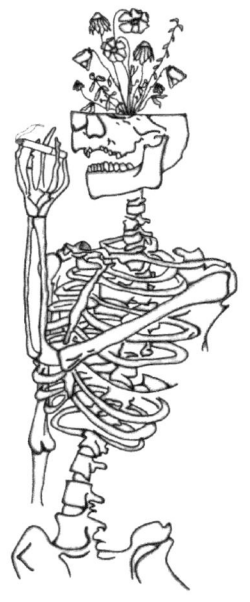

Estate.

Acquaintances with Mother, we were too young.
Too young to mind, with wild painted across our tongues.
Too young to care that spring was just blooming in our minds.
Fields not yet tended to; dry soil is where we spent our days.
Morphing hours into years, we drew up onto four,
of destroying gardens.
Reasons why I took two for myself are deep
in the flower graveyards.
Letting that young boy run through grass taller than inches,
Happens to be, to this day, of where I'll keep you.
That river ran a while, before never finding the ocean.
Too young, too much time, the bed is now empty.
With only carvings left in the stones I once skipped.
I'll visit the rapids that used to rage, from time to time.
Solely to thirst for the life now swimming in that tarn,
Lying deep in the mountains of my soul.

Withdrawals.

Nobody wants it.
Everyone craves it.
It's like that drug,
Shoot it up.
Burn it down.
Smell it good.
Taste it the next morning.
Notice how love and drugs are needed?
They are everything you were,
Nothing I ever wanted you to be.
It's like you're stuck in my throat.
Clawing your way out with my heart.
Leaving memories scratched into my esophagus.
Burning from the aftertaste of reasons why
I wasn't good enough for you.
Absence of you may be in my heart,
But never in my head.
I guess you could call it motivation.
To be nothing you ever needed,

And everything you ever wanted.

Illicit Falls

Illegal, Forbidden, Clandestine.

Confessions.

God, forgive me as I tell you about something you created.
You did so well drawing that jaw and picking the color of the eyes.
But Satan won as he placed alcohol and cigarettes on his breath.
He was taught so well how to run his fingers
across my skin to make it shiver.
I can't help but feel that internal hand drag me closer,
as his smirk forces me to my knees.
Forgive me God, as I swear to you,
that you put him here to drive me insane.
Thoughts leaking from this pretty little mind,
as parts of him leak from this not so pretty little mouth.
He takes the place of the soul momentarily,
as he fills this shell of a body with himself.
God, please forgive me, as I scream your name
while he forces my eyes to the back of my skull.
These words may have been dug from the depths of hell,
But he takes me to heaven as he breathes heavily on my thighs.
God, forgive me, for making your beautiful creature, my favorite *sin*.

Room #212

There are small hole in the wall places.
Places where you took parts of me, for yourself.
If the camera footage was rewound,
Stolen kisses,
Butt grabs,
Hand holding,
Would be spotted.
Trying to identify the robber,
because my heart was taken there.
That old comic bookstore,
Cheap hotel rooms,
Parked car jam sessions,
Expensive loud bars.
If you took all the pieces, you posses
Picked from the puzzle of me,
From these dark insignificant places,
You'd be able to see the picture of my love,
Only for you.

To Her.

I understand why you said your vows.
I know why you looked, and fell, just as I did.
Forgive me, as I succumb to your life.
I hate every part of me that yearns for him.
I hate the way he looks at me and I melt.
I hate the way he grabs my thighs,
as we drive to pointless destinations.
I hate the way we sing along to the most known tunes.
But what I despise the most,
is that I cannot lie and tell you that I hate him.
We share the same love, for a similar shadow.
I am sorry for stealing parts of him that you never saw.
You must understand why.
I am not sure which is worse.
That we share the same skin under those sheets,
Or that I am not big on caring.
Secrets are running thick and call me sick for drinking it up.
I apologize in advance, for the heartbreak to come.
Both to you and me.
Because I know, one day you'll come to claim what's yours.

Aquatic Respiration.

Have you ever loved a pair of eyes so much,
    that the skin they reside in becomes art?
Their soul dancing behind that color circling a black hole,
    becomes your favorite show
Goosebumps that rise with the cold of the night,
    becomes your favorite texture.

Have you ever loved a human being that you couldn't keep?
    You can't stop yourself from loving as deep as the ocean,
        knowing the pressure of the depth will eventually
kill you.
    I am good at swimming, so I'll tread that water,
        until I can no longer.
        Just don't save me when I drown,
        I am not one to be rescued.

Hymn of Love.

When your fingers take strings and turn them into music,
it echoes through my soul.
With ears recording the notes to playback when I am starving.
Starving,
For nothing but your voice, singing my favorite songs.
Tell me, how can ten fingers and one voice
play the life back into a soul?
This is my Novocain,
that numbs the rest of the world.

Taste of Poetry.

The smell of coffee fills the empty room as you put the pot on. You've perfected just how I like it. Pour the creamer to add some color. I'll wake up to the sounds of your actions in the other room. An instant smile is created across my face. The warm scent of coffee reminds me of how much you love me. "Crawl back into bed with me", I say, as you walk in with mugs. The sound of sipping and laughter fills the empty room, just as the sun does. Touch me softly, but only to prove how close you are. Read me your poetry and I'll read you mine; deeper meaning in between each line. Tell me you love me. I promise I'll say it back.
These are the dreams I have; nothing special, except for the fact that you are mine in the simplest of ways.

Wishful Wishing.

Look at the couple, over there.
Sitting on the bench.
What about the ones holding hands and laughing?
What's a flashback, when it's to the future?
The one you can never have.
The one where you're him, and I am her.

Biting my tongue, to taste blood run down into my stomach.
Holding my breath, to feel the sting of need inside my lungs.
Letting this fire burn.
Burn so deep down within,
That my heart will reach its hands out to warm itself.
Keeping this secret, to see you next to me one more night.
Journal entries made day after day,
Just so I don't forget how you made me feel, for an instance in time.
What a thrill I feel when I know I'll never see you again.

Discussions with the past always start with the inevitable truth,
Of thoughts shouted into nothingness.
Empty sheets soaked with tears.
Inescapable arguments over the shoulder.
Just to end, where it all began.
Clockwise spin of the head,
To daze the reality of what is.
Kill enough time to catch the common cold.
The one with no cure, that numbs the whole soul.
Slip from the grasp, if dealt the right hand.
Speak the secret of how to run fast.
Kidnapped heart on the loose.
Dashing from the ruins, back to the past.
To the day the sun set, thinking all would last.

Selfishness.

    I wish I could let you go, the way a butterfly lands on my finger and flies away. I wish I was satisfied with admiring you from afar, like the stars in the sky on a clear night. I wish I could be happy watching you disappear, like the sun setting on a calm ocean, for other eyes to see.
    Something you love, compares differently to *someone* you love. The sun and stars you love to share with your favorite people. You, I'd like to keep for myself, for all eternity.

Tell me, will fate play us another hand?
A winning hand this time, please.
I never take shooting stars or coins tossed into still water lightly.
I'll hold my tongue.
Pocket that change.
Just to hold onto my wish a little longer.

Toxic Blood, Clean Mind.

Carefully picking you out of my life,
    like sorting what I don't like out of my salad.
Finally cleansing your fingerprints off my heart,
    like a criminal leaving a crime scene.
Sweating your kisses out of my skin by running so fast,
    the vision I have of you, blurs.
God, I reminisce of how I described my favorite sin to you,
    now, on this bathroom floor,
I am begging you to redraw him out of my mind,
    make me blind like I know love is.
Paint him the colors I don't admire,
    so, I remember his lines, like the ones I once did.
You told me someone has to want help,
    so today, I drove myself to rehab.
Losing 170 pounds from the withdrawals off my shoulders.

    Don't get me wrong,

        I still hold that bottle at the neck.

          Inhale those fumes.

            But I'm cleaner than I have ever been.

Serpentine.

Stumbling over my skin that I seem to drag for miles.
Heart and soul not big enough to fill all the edges,
smooth all the wrinkles.
Cut the extra flesh, pin it to the wall.
A tapestry of what I used to be, decoration, trophy.
Proud to see all that I've let go of.
Less skin, but more room to pour all the love that I will drink up.
Shedding is what they call it,
When you lose the old and gain the new.
Like a snake, I've got new patterns you wouldn't recognize.
Stand outside that cage, tracing my new design.
I may be beautiful, but you're lucky that glass
is in between you and me.

Comparison Kills.

When he left,
    I could breathe easier.
The water he held my head under, no longer filled my lungs.
When you left, the trees no longer gave me oxygen
    and my breath was stolen.
Watching him walk out the door,
    was watching myself burn my suicide note.
Watching you walk through the doors,
    was watching the sun setting into a cold night.
These are the differences between
    surviving in a dying world,
    and *thriving* in a daydream.
Thank you,
    for *dancing* with my soul,
        walking with my body,
            and *falling* with my heart.

Trivial Pond

Inessential, Superficial, Paltry.

Worst Parts.

His skin leaves DNA traces that dance with mine.
Twirling and turning my reflection into distortion.
I want to steal the worst parts of him,
To mold and burn into the best parts of me.
Tell me why you bite your nails,
Or your deepest inner critic thoughts.
Then, *maybe,* I'll tell you why I write.

You Could Call This… Regret.

I'll make my own cloud nine,
with the fumes from the toxins, I breathe.
I'll make a home from these unfamiliar sheets I lie in.
With nothing to hide my vulnerability,
But these blue socks and dim lights.
Imprints of sweat left on those light-colored sheets,
Reflect how I am comfortable, being uncomfortable.
Whispers of what I want to hear when the sun is sleeping,
Scream into my left ear the next morning.
Making cringe ride up my spine,
Causing the bass to hit a little too hard.
Drowning out what I feel on the inside,
Like Novocain on my soul.

Insipid Stream

Vapid, Tasteless, Halfhearted.

Hands.

The first thing I touch when I see you,
    meeting you.
The last thing I feel, when you leave,
    losing you.
Gentle, but screaming with dominance.
Lines, to carry your identity.
Scars, add to your bio.
Silently, speaking loud words.
Underrated, as your fingers puzzle into mine.
Overlooked when you engulf mine in yours.
Between rocks and crashing waves,
Floating on the rough.
Fingers used as brushes to create art,
While dragged across my collarbone.
Palms portrayed as safety, while crossing the busy street.
Mine will show you where I have been.
Yours will show me where I am going.
So, sit with me, in this dark place.
Lie your hands into mine and let's read the creases that tell our futures.

Adrenaline Surge.

As muscled legs lift tattooed arms to reach for the sky,
Palm trees whoosh by.
That blue car driving through a paradise, with holes in the roof.
Worry seems to escape the mind.
Ocean meeting sand,
Sand meeting pavement,
Pavement meeting the streets that lead to the rest of your life.
On the edge of land.
On the edge of loving you.
On the edge of death,
I've never felt more *alive*.

Writer's Block.

Words; my most powerful weapon.
Harnessing a group of letters into feelings.
So, tell me why my weapon becomes non-lethal,
When you step into the room?
Gasping for bullets, suffocating under speechlessness.
Only to discover a bomb.
The kind that flattens trees and shakes the atmosphere.
Not looking to aimlessly drop but lighting the fuse anyway.
As sharp as a dull knife.
As poisonous as the oxygen expanding our lungs.
Comprised of three little words and embraced with passion.
Hoping the aftermath blooms a garden
fruitful enough to feed the heart.
Words; as a poet I should be superior in the way I present them.
So, tell me why it took ninety-one words
to spell out the fact that I love you.

I shouldn't have let you in.

You didn't do anything wrong.
My shadow of trauma followed you in,
and impolitely took a seat next to you.
Should have kept the door locked.
I can't take my eyes off you, with it in my peripheral.
How do I make it go away, but keep you here?
I don't want you to leave, but damn I want it gone.
I shouldn't have let you in.
I am tired of being on edge.
Glancing to the side.
Jumping at every sudden movement.
Should have stayed lonely.
Screaming silently in my head, as laughter belts out my mouth.
Holding back tears as you move closer, as it moves through me.
I built my house, fixed it up, and rid it of toxins.
I shouldn't have let you in.
Should have kept the door locked.
Should have stayed lonely.
I could have been fine, easing into life numb.
I shouldn't have let you in.
Needing you like the fumes I inhale.
I shouldn't have let you in.
Asking me what is wrong with myself.
I could have been fine.
Angry for no reason.

Angry at myself, taking it out on you.
I don't want this to **d i v i d e** us.
I shouldn't have let you in, now I can't let you leave.

Celestial Tarn

Heavenly, Godly, Immortal.

You Walk on a Rhythm.

I'll never let you know it.
How the way you walk,
speaks of a foreign language that only I took the time to learn.
Your voice carries a tune,
In a way that shakes my core with innocent pleasure.
Damaged from the weather,
Your eyes are cracked doors, letting me peer into your soul.
Reading behind the lines,
Burning cover to cover.
Feeling the fibers of our connection in depths so deep,
I can play them like a violin.

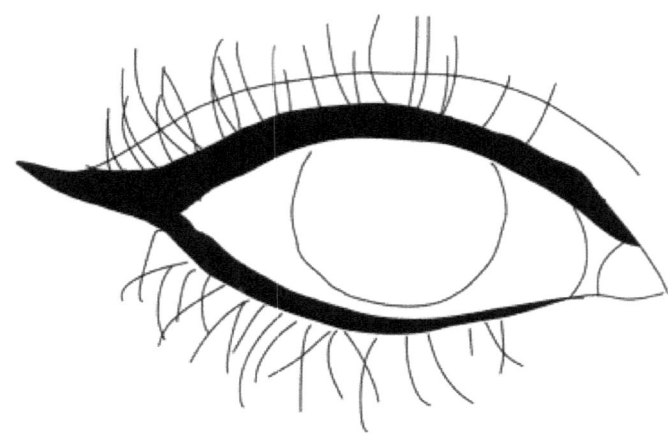

Kissing; Exhaling.

With time passing slower than the hands ticking on the clock,
Your fingerprints made impressions on her vulnerability.
Speaking of how to alter her body
on that pedestal to fit in your blurry vision.

Impenetrable by all, but the moon.
The earth shook as she showed her face.

Frozen in the wake,
she breathed all of who she was going
to be in the mouth of a familiar stranger.

Allowing the finally faced half of this lifetime
to reveal mountains she concealed.
Worlds collided.

Galaxy Merger.

Simplicity of bones covered with oversized sweaters,
when Mother faced away from the warmth.
Realization floods the room,
as flashes of time, not yet spend, presents itself at the door.
From afar, the eye would paint two skeletons welded with love,
Sitting in that booth.
Microscopically close, crack the dimensions into depths
Of galaxies reaching across to conjoin.
Intimacy boiling on the skin,
As love dances under the bridge of piercing eyes.
Blink away the canvas and go on through the sun,
Remembering how masses of two, collided as one,
sitting in that booth

Peruvian Love.

Our souls bouncing off the atmosphere,
Reflecting the city lights.
Our bodies running through streets,
Free and trapped by eyes.
Hair tangled with the spoken language,
As they mumbled about the reckless.
Replay it for the mind, in slow motion,
Swear by every detail.
Burned in like an old CD,
Skipping with scratches of adrenaline.
We twirled with love,
As our bodies played with lust.
Adventure became our wall less home,
As the city became our playground.

Pariah Delta

Outcast, Untouchable, Undesirable.

Grail.

A book in my hands, with the weight of all my dreams.
Pages so thick, punishing to reach the back cover.
Mockery of myself, pretending these poems are foreign.
Craving to taste each stanza on another's tongue.

Soon, the crowd will replace different versions of me.
Optimistically, snapping fingers, instead of crude comments.
Vulgar and innocent, warp the other's definition to stain these words.
Variety of significance, spoke between the lines.

Mirrored expressions to paint in the brain.
Moving words, oh so still, on the white.
Tread carefully through the cursive, of who I was.
Blaring my words between eyes and ears.
Grasp the growing pains of my origin.
As it has emerged from the vignette of youth.

The Night I Dreamt.

The night I slept for days, I dreamt of dying.
Forwards in my life, backwards in my death.
Hallways were a likeness, to what I thought I knew.
Heaven was occurring,
physical in dimensions I thought I couldn't know.
White was the vision, as my steps were into depths.
Walking on anything but my feet, submerged upwards.
Grounds morphed into clouds as the rain fell from below.
Destinations were far within reach and close on the map.
The soul was pure, but the skin was earthy.
Decorated with sins and washed with ink.
Images of who I was, melted into the energy I belonged to.

Your embodiment.

Year after person, the dirt and dust build up.
No dry cleaners open, no washing machine available,
To clean the dirtiest parts of a human, the soul, your innermost self.
Fingerprints are permanent, scars never heal with band aids to cover.
How do you wipe clean what's below the surface?
Endless tears, sweat stuck from that run, carved words from poetry.
Your soul is your advertisement to the world, who will you let see?

Contradictory.

Skipping through life with dragging feet.
Smiles so big, in an upside-down world.
Piercing knowledge shines through closed eyes into an empty cell.
Twenty-two years of performing in a vacant auditorium.
Cheers echoing from some place distant.
Curtains so dark, to the side I like to reside.
Demons raid, as happiness cowers in the corner.
What's left of it, anyway.
Daydreaming to a world my thoughts love to destroy.
Imagination escaping into itself.
A body given by God, is left behind to search.
Seeking a celestial body with non-existent colors.
My mind picking wildflowers; regrowing her garden.
While souls of galaxies shake my hand, introducing me to stars.

Sanctuary.

Desire sits where versions of him stood.
Designing his soul to style the new guests he invited in.
Doors so heavenly as the dim lights hid the mess of comfort.
Deity: he was worshiped in haven he considered safe.
Desolate resides in the sanctuary filled with characters he created.
Demise haunts the couch as her silhouette stains the cloth.
Defaced skeletons roam the ghostly territory.
Demons left for him to tend to.
Death strikes at every soft corner; keep it at bay.
Daunting are the walls he briefly empowered.
Drowning in empty space that echoes serenity.
Determined to redesign the confinement where, momentarily,
Utopia occupied his sanctuary.

Self Sever.

Living in a perpetual state of homesickness.
Looking to the moon to meet eyes with places I belong.
She's up there, playing hopscotch across stars.
Grown two sizes too big, Earth no longer fits on my feet.
Atmosphere crowding my brain, needing to breathe nothingness.
She's not here; surfing the rings of Saturn.
She painted the canvas of Jupiter, just to make me jealous.
Gravity shielding me from places, I can almost smell.
Dreams of her visions, to show me the galaxies I'll never visit.
Weighing down Pluto, she's waiting there.

Deluges That Feed All

What Is Needed, Will Flood.

I don't think I'm a good poet. It's not because I don't like my poems; I fall in love with the words I write. It's not because the old ones contain my past loves, or because trauma loves to be the main character.

It's because I want to write about my mom, how she is my rock. I want to write about the way water rolls over sand. How paint pursues can perfectly glide over canvas to create unworldly art.

How my aunt gave birth to a child that loves me dearly. How I serve my country in this uniform, proudly. I want to write about beings, and Mother Earth. How music literally vibrates my soul.

Forcing my hands to make bliss a guest character in my words is a skill I have not yet conquered. *Yet.*

Lost and Free.

Foreign in a beautiful place, is being lost within a map.
Street signs that lead us everywhere; nowhere.
Smoke and music fill the air while breathing
in each other's laughter.
With no intention of finding the destination,
As the journey of being lost, here, is beautiful in itself.

The Profound.

Waves take days and roll them into weeks.
Time is relative; no one cares what day it is.
Horizons disappear with the blue on blue.
Roots pulled up like weeds, sailing to no man's land.
Humor is used as a conduit, to hide the dark.
While uniform is used to disguise the individuality.
One body, part of something bigger.
"Be proud," they say,
But can I tell you about the silent tears?
How do I speak about the empty laughter?
Borderline mechanical, with too much emotion.
Where's home?
It's not that metal I sleep on.
Nor the embrace of familiar skin.
Falling in love with what pushes me to insanity,
is why my heart is in the ocean.
Deep at the bottom, like lost treasure.
Feet on the ground, puts my head in the clouds.
Don't ask me why I'm different.
Why I don't laugh the same.
Why I converse on another level.
I have learned to embrace
my personal darkness and conquer my light.

No one admires the stem of a flower,
the trunk of a tree.
Parts of the living, that provides the life.
Only the delicate, that catches the eye.
When Mother Nature gets lonely,
her harsh hands pick the pedals.
Questioning, love me, or love me not?
When the delicate is scattered on the ground, dead,
from the cold hands of picking,
People stare, still never turn to the living.
Set a fire Mother, warm your heart.
Gather the beautiful, harvest the living.
Sea of tears that nourish the delicate, only to drown the life.
Caressing the stem that grows inside.
Blossom your heart, to the delicate.
Waiting for someone to pull the roots attached to your soul,
just to plant them in their own world.

Unfortunately, My Future.

The age is approaching for my age to fresh.
A fresh life, with new skin.
Hair so feather thin, nails almost microscopic.
A new set of genes, warped with my love's.

Unknown is the nose, or the day to see with eyes.
Less than a year to fall in love, too much time.
Let the forgotten back room, become the center of gravity.
Filled with clouds, stuffed into pink cloth.

Let's perform the dance to create this life.
Fear sets in, as incapability might come knocking.
Caress each millionth piece, as it might win the race,
but no first-place prize to be given.

Fog leaks from the dusty cloth as it settles in the empty walls.
Ghostly laughter echoing from piece three of our set.
Unused love spilling for no young soul to drink.
So, let's get drunk on what's left in the bottle,
Because honey, it's just you and me.

Walls half built.
No windows or locked doors.
Unstable is the roof, ready to cave in.
No ability to house the body.
No food to feed the soul.
No heat to warm the heart.
Just the broken promise of maybe a home.

Obsession, addiction, desire.
All longing for something that makes you feel powerful.
That tight fitting clothing, clinging to the body I try to perfect.
Nothing but caffeine fills the stomach, I try to make flat.
Tears and sweat; both contain salt.
Tears are for the soul, sweat is for the body.
Muscle soreness is my high; feeding my body the want to feel more.
That reflection, once my enemy, now my favorite view.
Those tight jeans, once my motivation, now my favorite accessory.
My therapy session is standing inside a pair of running shoes.
Nobody speaks of those addictions that are good for you.
Maybe they should be advertised more than the ones that cover the hurt, instead of curing it.

Stained.

Torn to pieces.
Hear the fragments fall.
Jogged edges to cut the ones who try.
Try to piece them back together.
Don't touch the glass.
Don't tie the bow around what you claim as your masterpiece.
Leave the blood stains.
Remembrance of who once tried to touch.
A red stained glass to look through.
Perfect windows sitting in broken walls.
One piece to make all the heads turn.
Abandon the scraps for the sun to shine through.
With no one to watch.

I have found a bench,
that seems comfortable enough to lay my life on.
The weather is cold, and the wind is howling.
The closest warmth is the burning world, light years away.
Reflection of flames, flash in the tear rolling down my cheek.
It feeds the crumbling ground below me.
With each moon phasing by, it remains dark.
I stay shackled to this bench, watching the stars burn away,
Finding the end of endless.

My Monster Has a Name.

Pain creeps up from underneath my bed,
Like a monster, knowing all my weaknesses.
It's dark; can't make it go away.
So, I pull the sheets back and let it crawl in with me.
It brings ice to chill my skin, even under the blankets.
This twin bed can't contain both a soul and a monster.
Midnight battles: it victoriously rolls on top.
Pain and laughter shaking to my core.
God, make it stop.
Tears soak the bed, make up stains the sheets.
Feeding the monster.
Stories never mention how demons sneak into your bed.
Absorb into your brain.
Sink into your skin.
Sleep is the only paralysis.
Let the sun rise and face the day with the weight on your shoulders.
With falsity painted across the lips.
With gloom on the eyes, reflecting to the clouds.
Damn, these monsters make the head heavy.
Focus on the day.
Focus on the day.
Focus on the demons.
Eventually, the flowers planted in your mind, will push them out.
Just to create space for the new ones that poison your garden.

Paper Airplane.

A meaningless toy. Little paper airplanes are temporary thrill, representing something so big. Something that helps the escape. Leaving out all the important features. The means of flying; escaping, require more than what it can handle. Details help, how sharp can you make the crease? Each fold, place some dedication. Take your time, make the curves. When it's complete, admire it. So beautiful, sitting in your palm.
Time to fly.
Let's ride this escape. Loops and turns to show how you tried. Disappointment as it nose dives. Didn't go as far as you wanted? Didn't escape fast enough? Pick it up, check the creases. Make them sharper. Frustration as the realization of worthless overcomes. No escape from this world. No plane can take you far enough. Forget about it.
It will never fly.

Confluence.

Life with life within.
Death caused by life within.
Sources of it all, providing the subtraction.
Remembering who I was,
Knowing who I will be,
As the ripples distort the murky image of my statuette.
Standing over bodies of water, lying in the bed.
Studying the bony bends that curve with waves of skin.
Drowning in the wrinkles.
Breathing in the pheromone scents.
Palpitations carving skeletons of bodies lying in the bed of water.
Luna, lazily glimmer her reflections off limbs of rivers.
Reaching.
Stretching.
Colliding.
Tidal storms with shifts in the tectonic plates.
One body crashing into another.
Altered lives, pools left to remind how bodies laid in the beds.
Pieced apart masses left on the leaves, the sheets.
Empty riverbeds.
Depressed pillows left messy, as the sun beamed early.
Life dying in the shallow, but oh so deep beds.
While patient for when the craters show once again.

So, this is it.
What's below my skin.
You've flipped through each page of my dream.
Read each line of my soul.
Understood each word of my past.
My advertisement to the world, and I've chosen to let you see.
Be kind and hold these words dearly close.

CPSIA information can be obtained
at www.ICGtesting.com
Printed in the USA
BVHW021118260123
R14577700001B/R145777PG656438BVX00030B/30